Wheels to Ice: Born to Rise

AF652836

Verses Kindler Publication

Verses Kindler Publication.

Website: www.verseskindlerpublication.com

Wheels to Ice: Born to Rise

By: Mr. Aarush Tiwari

ISBN: 978-93-49532-71-7

1st Edition

Price: INR 199/$10

Disclaimer

Wheels to Ice: Born to Rise is authored by Aarush Tiwari. The entirety of this published work comprises the original content of the author, who has undertaken diligent efforts in its editing. The characters depicted herein may be fictitious or inspired by real events; however, they are not intended to cause offense or represent any prejudice against any caste or system. Any similarity to the names of actual individuals, locations, or institutions is purely coincidental and serves the narrative. The author bears sole responsibility for the originality of this work; the publisher assumes no liability thereof.

Index

This book is dedicated to my family — my deepest source of strength. To my late grandparents, Smt. K.L. Tiwari and Sri Dr. G.S. Tiwari, and to Smt. Pushpa Tiwari and Sri. Basant Kumar Tiwari, whose love guides me.

To my parents, Sonal and Amit Tiwari, for their support. And to my brothers, Archit and Suraj, for always being my quiet strength.

Preface

I never considered myself someone who would want to keep a diary. I always thought that diaries were for those who knew what was playing on their minds, had neat handwriting, and used beautiful words to express their feelings. I'm not like that. I use clumsy language. My thoughts take strange forms. Sometimes, when I write something down, it doesn't feel real the next day. Still, I continued to write.

It started with me documenting episodes of my friends cracking goofy jokes, the sound of my skates on the ice that one morning, and my feelings the first time I executed a jump I had been practising for a long time. I wrote about the late nights when I couldn't sleep because my mind was sprinting with opportunities and what-ifs and the early mornings when I wished to sleep an hour longer.

I envisioned this diary as a storehouse for those brief moments. However, an unforeseen event occurred. As I wrote more, it felt as though I was finally able to bring together the broken pieces of my life's puzzle. It became a story about believing in yourself, even when it seems like everything is falling apart, failing, and trying again. This book aims to discuss the realisation that difficult times don't indicate weakness but rather that you're growing. These pages now remind me of all the times I wanted to give up and the reasons I didn't. I recall the times when I was brave and the times when I was afraid. I see the friends who stood by me and the moments I stood alone but found a way to keep going.

I am aware that I am not the only person who has had this experience. Other young people—athletes, artists, and dreamers—have experienced the pressure of striving for greatness. This book is for anyone who has ever felt invisible, not good enough, or like their story didn't matter. It's for everyone who has ever been on the brink of something significant and been afraid to take the next step forward.

It's more than just a diary. It's a series of incidents that, when combined, tell an inspiring story of bravery, falling and rising, and hope.

Turn the page if you're prepared to enter my world and witness the behind-the-scenes activities, the messy parts, and the moments that made me laugh, cry, and persevere. Because this isn't just my story, it might be yours, too.

Acknowledgement

This book is not more than a collection of moments; it is a map of my heart. Each page carries indelible imprints of those who helped in tracing the journey and supported me through every breakdown, bruise, and breakthrough.

I'm deeply grateful to Ms. Deepti Vohra, Principal of DPS Vasant Kunj, for her support and belief in my journey beyond the classroom. Your kindness gave me space to grow without fear.

To Mr Azad Singh, our Sports Head—thank you for championing my efforts and always backing my pursuits.

To Jagmohan Sir and Bharti Rathi Ma'am—your quiet strength and support meant more than I can say.

To every teacher and Class Representative, I express my gratitude for your patience in helping me excel academically.

To my coach, Mr. J.S. Sahney—thank you for training me not for medals but for a purpose.

To my family—my backbone, soul, and biggest cheerleaders. This book is as much yours as mine.

To our publisher, Verses Kindler Publication, for believing in my voice and helping me share it with the world.

And to every young skater, dreamer, or artist out there—you belong. You matter. Keep going. Dream big. Skate harder. Never dull your spark.

A Note from Sourav Ganguly

Let me be genuine: I don't generally read books written by teenagers. Especially athletes. Most of the time, you expect the typical—"I trained hard, I gave up a lot, I love my country." And yes, all that is important. But Aarush's book? It hit differently.

This isn't a list of accomplishments or a polished PR story. It's a real, raw, and truthfully funny take on what it means to chase something no one else around you understands. Aarush talks about falling—literally and emotionally—and how he keeps getting back up. That, to me, is more powerful than any medal.

What stood out the most? His voice. It's not melodramatic. It's not overly serious. It's just unpretentious. And that honesty makes you want to keep reading, whether you've ever worn skates or not.

Aarush, I respect what you're doing—on the ice and the page. Keep writing, keep pushing, and keep proving that sport in India isn't just about cricket or track. It's about belief.

You've got something special here. And I'm glad I read it.

— Sourav Ganguly
Ex- India Team Captain

A Special Note

When we talk about sporting superiority, we frequently concentrate on medals, rankings, and records. But sometimes, the most powerful contributions don't come from the podium. They come from the pages of a book that has texts written with resolve to achieve one's dreams and passion .

This book isn't just a memoir. It's a rupture. A reminder. A voice rising from a frozen corner of Indian Ice Sport to say: *I am here. And I have something to say.*

Aarush Tiwari has lived a story that most people can just imagine and even fewer would have the courage to tell. As President of the Ice Skating Association of India, I have seen firsthand the challenges our athletes face: not just for victory, but for visibility. Aarush has met those battles with grit, grace—and now, with words.

His writing is not polished for effect. It is meticulous because it is true. It is bold, funny, aching, and alive with the kind of honesty you rarely find in any genre—let alone in sport.

This book is not just about skating. It's about daring to exist in a space where no one handed you a map. And then having the vision to chart one for others.

My compliments to Aarush who through this has created a starting point for countless others.

For us you are not just a skater , You are a storyteller. A builder. A quiet revolution on blades.

We are proud of you.

And more importantly—we are listening.

— Amitabh Sharma

President, Ice Skating Association of India (ISAI)

Vice President , Asian Skating Union.

Executive Council Member, Indian Olympic Association (IOA)

Foreword

There are students you watch from a distance. And then, once in a while, someone comes along who carves out a quiet, unexpected place in your memory. Aarush Tiwari was one of those.

Our paths crossed under unusual circumstances. During the 18th National Ice and Figure Skating Competition, his entry had missed the official deadline and couldn't be processed in time by the association. It was a challenging situation, and I was approached with a simple request: to consider letting him in. I didn't know much about him then—just that he was young, eager, and had come a long way for the chance to compete. I said yes. In retrospect, the gesture was insignificant at the time, but it signalled the commencement of the unimaginable.

What transpired next was not merely a show or a competition but a path of blossoming that I have had the honour of witnessing since that day. Aarush didn't come with noise or reputation. He came with quiet resolve. In a country where ice sports barely find space in conversation, let alone infrastructure, he kept showing up—humble, determined, and ready to learn.

This book is not written to showcase medals or records. It's written with honesty and heart. Aarush has captured the solitude of training, the struggle of self-doubt, and the quiet triumphs that don't always get applause—but build character.

Reading his story, I saw not just the skater—but the person behind the blades. Someone who chose to reflect instead of boast, someone who dared to put his journey into words—not for glory, but for truth.

This book is for every young dreamer struggling to make their way in a system that isn't built for them. And I am proud—not just of the athlete Aarush has become—but of the voice he has found and the courage it takes to share it.

— J.S. Sahney,

General Secretary of the Ice Skating Association of India

About the Author

Aarush Tiwari is an emerging Indian figure skater and storyteller who started at the age of 3.5 years with a pair of roller skates and a wish to fly.

From cement floors to the stylish performances on international ice, Aarush has emerged as one of India's youngest and most promising skating stars. His achievements include gold medals at the 18th, 19th, and 20th National Figure and Speed Ice-Skating Championships—tying up the national championship for three successive years, and the All India Open Roller Skating Championship 2023 win and first ranks in Interschool Championships. Globally, he has achieved 5th position at the Asian Open Figure Skating Trophy 2023 and Thailand Open 2024, a bronze medal at the Asian Open Figure Skating Trophy 2025 in Manila, Philippines, and the distinction of being the sole Indian boy who was nominated by the Olympic Council of Asia for the illustrious Asian Youth Camp at Harbin, China.

But Aarush's life is more than medals. Off the ice, he's a reflective, inquiring mind who loves books, journaling, analyzing skating videos, and strawberry sundaes. A Harry Potter fan, quiet nooks, and sudden laughter, Aarush reconciles toughness with emotional complexity.

This is his debut book, an honest, honest, and very sincere account of pursuing greatness in the midst of growing pains, pressure, and purpose that accompany it.

Aarush Tiwari isn't skating to win; he's skating to inspire, to fit in, and to create something much bigger than himself.

Aarush receiving the medal for the Asia Open.

Entry 1: Flying on the Ground

I've never actually written a diary before, but Mumma says that some stories are worth remembering—particularly those that change you a little.

She gave me this notebook and said, "One day, you'll thank me."

And she's correct. Because if there's one thing I never want to forget, it's the first time I saw people skating. It was the moment that defined my life and would change me in ways beyond my wildest dreams.

This diary? It's about that.

About how a tiny spark turned into something I never let go of.

I was about four and a half— the kind of kid who ran around pretending to be an aeroplane, loved Mumma's food and asked "Why?" fifty times a day.

I remember this memorable day distinctly. We were in Malviya Nagar Market- a place usually full of colourful shops, ice cream stalls, and street dogs chasing each other. But that day, I saw something else—something that would unexpectedly change the course of my life.

Mumma was busy shopping for something, and I was busy being a fighter jet. "Zoom, Zoom!" I was yelling while running out of the shop. And that's when I saw a big, shiny rectangle on the ground. It immediately reminded me of what I had seen in my storybooks and cartoons — like a place where I would maybe see superheroes!

"What is that, Mumma?" I asked her, my eyes wide in wonderment as I indicated at it.

"That's a roller skating rink," she said.

I tugged on her clothes to take me closer. It looked like such a fun place. Many other children like me were laughing and zooming by like rockets. They also fell, but they were still laughing. Some of the older kids were moving so fast that I thought they were actual superheroes.

I asked, "Mumma! Are they flying?!"

She laughed and said, "No, beta. They're skating."

Mumma didn't rush me, and we waited for a long time. She told me later that my face that day was something she'd never forget — like I had stars in my eyes because they were so excitedly bright.

I kept watching and listening to the sounds coming from the rink — the wheels, the laughter, the wind swishes. After a while, I just sat on the ground watching my favourite movie.

When we got home, that excitement followed me. I ran to find my sandals and tried sticking bottle caps to them — that's how I remembered the skates looking. Of course, they didn't work like the real ones! Even if I couldn't skate, I would swish my feet while walking and try to make those sounds, imagining I was doing what those kids were doing.

I even had to ask Mumma several times to remind me of the word before I finally got it.

Skating.

And once I got it, I never forgot it.

Whenever we returned to that market, I secretly hoped Mumma would take me by the rink. And whenever she did, my face lit up like Diwali lights. Every single time.

Back then, I was happy to see that fantastic place. But now I know what happened that day:

I saw my very first dream.

A dream I still have and always will.

Entry 2: Skates, Straps & Super Aarush

Do you remember those bottle caps I taped onto my sandals as a kid? The "homemade skates" that made me fall more and skate less!

I'm thinking of the day I finally got the real deal.

Not plastic caps. Not fantasy. Real skates with actual wheels. The kind that glides when you get them just so — or throw you into the wall when you don't. I still have the ache in my cheeks from smiling that much.

So here's what happened that day:

Mumma said we had to go shopping. I grumbled a bit for I wanted to stay home and play. I thought it was going to be one of her usual errands. But then she took a different turn. Suddenly, we were standing in front of a huge sports shop. On the glass were pictures of bats, balls, rackets, and all kinds of gear. My eyes widened. I didn't walk in; I floated.

And then — I saw them. A giant rack full of skates. Big ones. Small ones. Some had thin wheels, and some had thick ones—every colour you can imagine. My heart started beating faster.

I turned to her slowly and asked, "Are you... are you buying me skates?"

Mumma smiled and nodded.

"YAYYY!" I shouted, probably loud enough for the whole market to hear.

One of the salespersons at the came to help me try them on. The first pair squeezed my toes—way too tight. The second was too floppy—like chappals on wheels. I started to feel a bit sad. What if nothing fits?

But then the third pair slid on like they were meant just for me.

Red and black. Shiny. Strong. And very, very cool.

I stood up in them and remember thinking, "I feel as tall as Papa!"

I took one tiny step — and crashed. Flat on the shop floor.

The salesperson chuckled and said, "That means they fit well!"

Mumma smiled and said, "We'll take them."

She also purchased a helmet, knee pads, elbow guards, and wrist guards. It was like I was preparing for a space mission.

When we arrived home, I didn't wait for a second. I dropped my bag, yanked on the gear, and put on the skates in the living room.

First attempt: Fell straight into the sofa.

Second attempt: Knocked over the mop bucket.

Third, I slipped so badly that I ended up flat on the floor like a chapati.

I was getting tired, sweaty, and a little frustrated. Just then, I flopped onto the sofa for a quick break. Papa was in the drawing room watching an old India vs. Pakistan cricket match. I wasn't really watching—my brain was still spinning with skating attempts—but suddenly, I heard MS Dhoni on the TV saying, "Don't be afraid of failure. It's the first step to success."

I smiled at my bruised elbow and whispered, "Thanks, Mahi bhai." It felt like he was talking to me. That was all I needed. I got up. Took a deep breath. Tightened the straps again.

Fourth attempt: I wobbled and slid. But I didn't fall.

I was actually moving for real.

"YES!" I shouted. "Mumma! I'm moving!"

She clapped from the kitchen like I'd just won a gold medal. Papa smiled and said, "Careful, champ."

I spent the next hour skating in short zigzags around the room. I still fell. A lot. But I laughed more. My arms were sore, my knees were red — but inside, I felt like a superhero.

That night, after I went to bed, I wiped my skates clean with a cloth and left them beside my pillow—yes, on the bed, not on the floor.

I went to bed with exhausted legs, sore arms, and a happy heart. I no longer felt afraid. Okay—perhaps a little bit. But mostly? I felt prepared. Like something incredible had just started.

Entry 3: Before Skating Took Over

There was a brief time when I didn't spend every minute thinking about skates. Skating didn't start as a calling. It started as curiosity, then became comfort—and eventually, something like home. It is now the thing that I love and feel most excited about. But skating wasn't always my everything.

I used to love *a lot* of other things before I discovered it. (Or maybe before it discovered me.)

Let's start with football. I was consumed by it. I was always ready for a game, to run and sweat and feel the thrill of the ball at my feet.

The instant the bell in school rang for break, I'd sprint to the ground, hoping for a good game. On weekends, you'd find me on the neighbourhood field, the ball at my feet, the laughter of my friends echoing. Time? Didn't matter. Weather? Didn't matter. Even if the heavens outstretched and the rain poured like cats and dogs, I'd be slipping in muddy puddles. We didn't care if it was a mucky field or a parking lot. As long as we had a ball and something to use as goalposts — water bottles, shoes, schoolbags — my friends and I were ready. I wasn't the team captain or the goal scorer. But, I was the one who ran the most; "like a headless chicken," Papa used to say. I enjoyed the running, the uproar, and the teamwork, and when I was passed the ball, I felt like I was a part of something meaningful—even if I immediately tripped!

Then came badminton.

I decided badminton would be "my thing" after Papa gave me this superb white and blue racquet. I decided that badminton would be *my thing* the day Papa gifted me a shiny red racquet. It looked so cool that I felt like a champion just holding it. I spent hours trying to beat my record by keeping the shuttle in the air without letting it drop. I think my highest score was 21 or maybe 12. Okay, fine, possibly 8. But still! It felt like a world record to me. The funny thing is that I always did better whenever I was alone. The shuttle would float like magic. But the moment someone was watching — poof! Down it went. Every. Single. Time.

There was drama, of course. Thus, I signed up for everything, including school plays, class skits, and festival programs. I adored the stage. The lighting. The outfits. Even the false beards that kept falling off my face. I had a thrilling time performing on stage. It was a mix of excitement, fear, and pure enjoyment. My mother always helped me in practising my lines. She forced me to say them clearly, loudly, and with "emotion!" Occasionally, while she used to be stirring daal in the kitchen, we acted together.

So, yes, I was busy with acting, football, and badminton before I started skating. I also believed that I was content—until the market day. The gleaming rink, the wheels whirring, and children flying across the floor as if it were the most typical thing ever.

Roller skating rolled into my life and became the hub of my universe in an instant. It wasn't only a new passion; it was as if I was finding a new me. While I threw myself into this thrilling journey, my other passions—badminton, football, and drama—found their place naturally decreasing in my day-to-day life.

But upon reflection, I see how they paved the way for skating in their respective ways. Badminton taught me concentration and accuracy, translating to focus during complicated skating performances. Football encouraged me to feel speed and quickness, which naturally translated to the rink. And drama? It taught me to feel confident in performing and balanced enough to stay poised—after all, freezing like a tree on stage is more challenging than it appears! Every experience, in some way, set the stage for my path into skating.

Skating isn't just something I do for fun anymore. I feel like I'm a part of it, and it's a part of me. It's nothing like the role-playing games I used to participate in—like pretending to be a superhero on a mission with my cousin or acting as a police officer charging toy robbers. This feels natural.

It's not a pastime, but my life.

This is me.

Lights, laughter, and memories at Warner Bros. – a family moment straight out of a movie

Entry 4: The Day I Thought I'd Fly

Skating didn't begin the day I first saw it. It really started the day Mumma made it happen. Whenever I paused to gaze at the rink in Malviya Nagar Market, I assumed she was listening quietly. She had a plan, though. She said, "Be ready" one day. This week is when your skating lessons begin. It turns out that Mumma was doing it while I was dreaming. She had visited the market, talked to the coach, and inquired about everything, including schedules, equipment, costs, safety, and even the type of socks I would require. Mum arranged for my enrollment, covered the costs, and created a list of the equipment I would need, including skates, a helmet, pads, a water bottle, a towel, and more. To accompany me, she abandoned her work. She showed up for me. And at the time, I had no idea how much that meant.

Now, let's talk about the actual skating part. I felt energized. Buzzing. My brand-new red-and-black skates were shining like superhero boots. But as I was ready to leave, Mumma said, "Helmet." "Knee pads" "Pads for the elbows." "Guards at the wrist." And a "No arguing" expression. I had the impression of being a miniature astronaut. I moaned, "Mumma, how will I move at all in this?"

I didn't quite resemble those children I had watched zooming around at the rink. I resembled someone enveloped in bubble wrap. I longed to glide, not to bounce.

"Those things are holding me back!" I grumbled. She fixed me with a straight gaze and declared, "They're protecting you." I disapproved. I felt that they were not protecting me at all. But I wore them anyway.

We came to the little beginner's rink. It was smooth and shiny, packed with other children—some gliding, some falling, and some just standing still like statues.

I entered. Took a deep breath. Stepped forward. BAM! First fall. Right on the backside. I remained on the ground, blinking up at the ceiling. The coach approached me and grinned. "Good first fall," he said. I didn't know whether I was going to laugh or cry.

Second attempt: Stepped one, slid sideways, and crashed into the wall.

My helmet bumped, and I sat like a dazed potato on the floor. I stared at Mumma through the glass. She was grinning and cheering. Me? I was hot, hurt, and fuming. "These things you made me wear are making it more difficult for me!" I complained to her. She agreed, saying, "You won't fly if you're too afraid of falling. The gear lets you stand back up." I didn't say anything. But within my heart, I began to realize she was correct. So I went again.

Third attempt:

Push. Wobble. Arms out like a baby bird.

Still upright.

"MUMMA, LOOK!" I exclaimed.

She applauded like I'd performed a triple spin (I'd travelled two metres, maximum). But at that instant? I was flying. Later, my legs ached, my knees were red, my hair was sweaty, and I had the biggest smile. I didn't fly like those children I'd seen in the market that afternoon. But I flew enough for me.

And you know what I realized afterwards?

I'd always thought that superheroes wore capes. You know, Spiderman. Batman.

And obviously, Pavan Putra Hanumanji is the OG superhero.

But I do know now that not all superheroes wear capes. Some wear dupattas. Make their son put on knee pads and helmets to keep him safe, even if he doesn't want to. They just always know the correct thing to say after low marks in an exam. And one hug from them solves every problem.

And I have such a superhero in my life- my Mumma.

There's no one like her. She's my guiding light, and my inspiration. Mumma is truly one of a kind.

Entry 5: Life in Every Direction

After that initial day at the rink—when I tripped, fell, and sailed for only two metres—Mumma applauded and appreciated me for my early efforts. That changed everything in me—not all at once, but gradually, like emerging from a long siesta. I did not realize it then, but that little step encouraged me to go on and continued telling me to improve. It was not solely about skating. I felt I had discovered a new aspect of myself that I did not realize existed.

But what about before that?

Before skating, I had a hundred small dreams. They just came and went from my mind, like passing clouds in the sky. They hung around for a while and then drifted off like paper boats after rain.

Every day felt like a new adventure, bursting with imagination and endless possibilities. As I mentioned earlier, I was already involved in cricket, drama, and anything that let me explore and express myself, so there was always something exciting to dive into.

The score was often forgotten on the school pitches as we kicked the football around. The joy was in the game, not in winning or losing.

I used to play cricket in the colony with a plastic bat and a rubber ball. The wicket was always somebody's scooter, and we had to stop the game every so often to apologize to an aunty whose potted plant had been struck — again.

At home, Papa and I used to play badminton. We'd place a net between two chairs on the terrace. The shuttlecock would take to the air and fall onto the roof, and we'd fling chappals at it to bring it down, crying with laughter until our stomachs ached.

There were no trophies, no dreams. I just enjoyed moving. I enjoyed the ecstasy of the game, that feeling of being fully alive, hearing the wind rushing past my ears, and the excitement of my heart pounding just because it could.

And then there was something else: drama.

In Class 1, I was cast in a small role during a school play. I wore a gold paper crown and spoke only two words. But when the crowd applauded, I felt something new — like I'd entered another world and somehow fit there. That feeling persisted. My parents enrolled me in the Sanjeev Datta Personality School, a famous institute to learn drama skills. I then began acting in my school's major shows and productions. I learned how to use silence, stand my ground on stage, look into an audience's eyes and move them.

People started saying I was a "natural." Thanks to my Class Teacher and principal, I was formally inducted into the school's Dramatics Society, and gradually, the theatre became what I loved most. For some time, I thought I'd be an actor.

But even then, inside, I didn't feel like I'd discovered 'the thing' for me yet.

The one thing that I couldn't get out of my mind.

The thing that made my heart pound harder than anything else.

Then, quietly, skating came into my life. It didn't come with a loud bang, thunderous or boom-like. It was soft, nearly invisible. It began when I stood behind glass, watching the other children whizz across Malviya Nagar market's ice rink. I observed them skate, trip, get up, and attempt to do it again. I didn't say much, but Mumma noticed a spark in me upon seeing that.

She always notices.

And so one day, she said, "Get set. Your training starts this week."

That is when my world changed.

From then on, skating wasn't an activity anymore. It was a feeling. A pull. A beat in my body I didn't know existed until I experienced it.

The games I played didn't come to a stop. I still enjoy acting. I still play cricket and badminton and run around like a storm when I can.

But skating changed.

Skating wasn't just about fun anymore — it was about belonging. It was about being part of a community of people with the same passion and dedication.

Skating made me more alert, more powerful, and more immersed. It made me realize the importance of doing what you love. It's not just a hobby; it's a promise that demands your whole heart and returns its own.

When I'm asked, "What do you want to become?" I don't shrug.

I respond clearly: "I want to skate."

I had many little loves before the wheels showed up and owned me.

But skating provided all of them with direction. It made all the random sparks within me — the games, the tales, the stage lights — into one constant flame.

Skating provided my dream with a name.

Entry 6: Skating Became Ours

My parents never needed an explanation. They understood everything long before I could find the words. They saw the transformation each time I approached the rink, in how I stood and leaned forward as if I were already gliding. My heart didn't race with fear but with something more profound—joy, fulfilment, and purpose.

Even in the early days, when my steps were uncertain and falls were frequent, they saw the signs. They knew this wasn't just a phase; it was becoming a part of me. And the most amazing thing? I never once had to explain it.

They could read it in my silence, how I carried my bruises and the quiet smile that followed each class. They didn't need words; they just knew. But Mumma was the first to stand behind me—and with me.

Skating began as a secret hope that felt like flying, even if I wasn't off the ground. I wanted to see what skating was all about. I tried to pass beyond observation, attempt, and study. And Mumma ensured that I could do all of these. She did it all, whether it involved finding the best coach, helping me prepare, or travelling with me to distant locations away from Delhi. Even the district-level competitions, where the venues and rinks weren't great, the waiting times were long, the summers were unbearably hot, and the cold reached us through our jackets. But she never once stepped back, even when the competition was tough and the conditions were challenging. She was always there—a steady pillar in my life.

It was her hands first, even for something as simple as tying the laces of my skates. I could fall if I made one mistake; a single missed strap could result in an injury. Additionally, injuries in skating happen—they don't ask for permission. She was aware of that. Nevertheless, she consistently returned, cheering, bringing extra socks and water bottles, and cheering me when I felt my confidence was dying.

Everything started to change as the game and I grew. The sport became increasingly challenging, the routines more complex, the contests fiercer, and I became more devoted.

Papa also stepped in at that point. He tells me the game began "graduating." And it's true—it was no longer just about skating. It was about mental toughness, discipline, thought, and reflection. Papa never hovered, but he was always there. He listened. Watched. And when he saw how dedicated I'd become, he engaged differently. Not just inquiring if I won, but asking: "What did you learn today?" "What's holding you back?" "What can we change together?" He became a guide — teaching me to think, plan, recover, and rebuild. He explained that supporting a child's dream is not merely being present but contributing to the mindset behind the dream. He and Mumma believed that achievement is not simply standing on a podium. It's also being able to get up again after you've fallen.

Speaking of my elder brother, Archit, he is my backbone and most adorable cheerleader. He never once asked me why I was taking this road. Archit Bhaiya only made me feel proud of my actions and thoughts—pushing me, giving advice, and cheering on each small win with the sort of delight that only someone who dearly loves you is capable of.

Soon enough, I realized something peculiar and lovely. I wasn't skating by myself anymore. My entire family had followed me into the rink — not on skates, but in spirit. They shared this dream with me. Every early-morning practice, every aching muscle, every medal, every defeat. It was all theirs. I could see it in their faces every time I got hurt. The triumph danced in their eyes every time I stepped onto a podium. They held the trophies with me. They draped medals around their necks, even just in the living room. And sometimes, when we speak of skating in the evening — of techniques, errors, routines — it seems there isn't only one skater in the house anymore. There are four. My dream wasn't mine for very long. It became ours — borne, guarded, and believed in by all of us. And perhaps that's what makes me skate harder each day.

Alongside the support from Mumma and Papa, my maternal grandparents play a vital role in my life. Since they first heard about my love for skating, my Nana and Nani began to sit in a quiet room. What would they do there? With eyes closed, prayer beads in hand, they'd whisper my name in every chant before I participated in a tournament. Their maala jaap was a powerful request asking for strength and guidance for me. They have always held the view and taught me that although skill is sharpened by practice, effort is transformed into success by God's will and elders' blessings. Their prayers are more than just customs; they are laced with immense love and faith. They carry me with their devotion, even though I'm the one skating. Their unspoken blessings have influenced my accomplishments and my decision to take up skating as a passion. It's a purpose that lives not just in my body but in the hopes and hearts of those who believe in me, even from the prayer mat, and it's a purpose that was shaped by their influence.

And then there is Suraj Bhaiya. He's our driver to most, but to me, he's been so much more. Right from the start, he's been part of my skating life—not by driving me to practices and competition, but by being present in every way. He's the one who videotapes my routines, closely examines them, and tells me what I need to work on. He reminds me to stretch, assists with my warm-ups, and ensures that all—I mean, all—from my skates to my stance is in order. Even when there's no competition on the horizon, he ensures that I do my exercises and keep my edge sharp.

There have been instances when I had to go to different cities or even foreign countries, and he couldn't accompany us. But that never deterred him from being involved. Mumma and Papa would record him sending me videos of my performance, and he'd respond with voice messages—what was good, what wasn't good, and how I could improve the next time. One time, before a crucial competition, Suraj Bhaiya's message helped me get the push I needed.

He always tells me, "Winning only counts if you've given your 100%." And if I haven't, he'll come out and tell me—not to make me feel bad—but because he believes in me. His rock-solid belief in my potential is a constant source of motivation.

He's a coach, a mentor who guides me through the ups and downs of skating, and a cheerleader who is always there to lift my spirits. He's like family who cares, and his role in my skating journey is irreplaceable.

In every stride, I carry the silent strength and blessings of my late Dadu and Dadi. Their unseen presence continues to guide me, helping me win medals, smiles, and pride for my parents, family, school, and every friend who walks beside me.

Friends who feel like home

Entry 7: The Delhi Drift

You know how people say, “One day you’ll laugh about this”?

Well, this is that “one day.” But back then? I thought the world was ending.

It was a special morning. I was all set for the skating tournament. My skates were shining. My backpack was loaded, and my hair was brushed. I had a banana and ensured my sports ID was duly draped over my neck.

Papa had to rush to the office to attend an urgent Board meeting while Mumma informed the driver to get the car ready. We were in the car early, driving through Delhi with the windows rolled down and Lata Mangeshkar singing softly on the radio. I was in good shape and spirits.

And then…the mobile phone rang. Mumma answered the call and put the device on speaker mode. It was Coach- — sounding far too energetic for that hour.

"Good morning, Mrs. Tiwari! Are you on your way?"

Mumma smiled graciously. "Yes, yes, we're almost there. Fifteen minutes more."

Coach paused. “That’s great! And you’re heading to the updated venue, right?”

Mumma froze. “Updated venue?”

My heart did a triple spin — without skates.

Coach sighed as if about to break bad news. "There was a change yesterday evening. Did you get the email? Aarush's session was rescheduled. He's not in the second half anymore — he's opening the event!"

Mumma's eyes blinked a million times in a second. "What?! No, we weren't informed! We're getting close to the old—uh, the initial location!"

The Coach remained unruffled, but we knew he'd prefer to scream into a pillow. "Hurry up. You might just make it."

And then it was like being in one of those action flicks — rerouting, seat belts clicking, watching the clock tick by. The vehicle couldn't accelerate any faster, and my head was whirling faster than any jump I'd ever taken.

At that moment, my heart dropped. Mumma didn't even speak.

I gazed at Mumma. She gazed back at me.

Then she went into full-blown Mission Impossible mode.

"Suraj Bhaiya!" she yelled to the driver. "Speed lagao. Fly the car if necessary. Just don't be late."

The driver nodded, flooring it like we were in a Bollywood car chase.

Except we were in Delhi. Auto-walas going across at random. A buffalo munching leaves on the divider. People arguing in the middle of the road as if it's their living room. Horns. Honks. Brakes. Dogs. More horns. Somewhere between mild hysteria and Mumma's fast-talk mumbling into the GPS, I did think:

"If I get away with this, maybe I deserve two medals today — one for skating and one for making it through this craziness."

After this, the real drama started: Wearing gear while the car was moving. Mumma managed to fix the helmet securely. But given the car bumping against the speed breakers, WHAP—it landed on my head.

Then she exclaimed, "Elbow pads!."

“Tighter!” she said. “No, looser! Aarush, stop moving!”

“I’M NOT MOVING, THE CAR IS!!”

Knee pads: one straight, one halfway up my thigh.

Wrist guards: one clipped, one dangling like a rakhi.

And the skates? She wrapped one on so tight my toes weren't feeling a thing. The other kept slipping off.

All while the car was jolting over potholes, and cows were greeting us (okay, maybe not greeting, but you get the idea).

And then, Mumma began reciting the Hanuman Chalisa.

Loudly.

Quicker than ever.

In between gear instructions.

“Bhoot pishach nikat nahi aave…”

“Aarush, lift your foot!”

“Mahavir jab naam sunave…”

“Bhaiya, ek baar horn bajaa dena please!” (Brother, please press the horn one more time)

I swear I almost expected Bajrang Bali himself to show up and airlift me to the rink.

Meanwhile, I was sweating, panicking, and whispering every single thing Coach had ever taught me:

“Bend your knees.”

"Eyes forward."

"Please don't fall flat."

We arrived at the venue in 7 minutes and 5 seconds (I was staring at the smartwatch like a bomb timer). I stumbled out of the car, resembling a half-packed suitcase.

Coach spotted me and blinked. "At least you made it," he said.

I nodded, too winded to even utter "Hello!"

And then I skated.

With mismatched socks. Helmet slightly askew. But I DID IT. WE DID IT.

Subsequently, Mumma embraced me and greeted, "We made it. Jai Bajrang Bali."

Her hands were trembling, but her eyes were beaming with pride.

We didn't merely endure a venue shift.

We conquered Delhi traffic.

We wore full skating attire in the back of a car.

We battled time, fear, potholes — and emerged laughing.

Frankly? That could have been my best warm-up yet.

On the way back home, Mumma finally called Papa.

He had been calling nonstop earlier when we were stuck in traffic. When I answered, he was half-panicked and half-praying.

"Are you alright?!" he asked. "Where are you now? Did you skate? Are you okay?!" He kept repeating, "My special darling boy, do you know how worried I was? I was calling all the Gods to keep you safe!"

I explained everything to him—the venue switch, the skating, and how we arrived on time. He fell silent instantly and whispered, "I'm proud of you." That made my chest all warm and fuzzy.

On the way home, Mumma said, "Want your favourite?"

And I didn't even have to tell her.

She turned straight toward the ice cream stand and got me my “strawberry sundae”—with crunchy nuts, vanilla chips, and extra of everything—the kind of treat that makes all the stress disappear.

As I sat there, legs still sore, sundae in hand, I gazed at Driver Dada in the front seat.

"Thank you," I said.

He turned around, smiled, and said jokingly, "Arre, medal toh mujhe milna chahiye!" (I should be the one receiving the medal)

And guess what? He wasn't mistaken. Because on that day, I understood something.

Success is not one man's alone.

Behind each victory are individuals who stop what they're doing, change their schedules, drive through insanity, hold your hand, lace your skates, or root you on. I skated that day. But countless others made it happen.

And that's what made it so unforgettable.

Entry 8: Before Coaching, There Was The Carpet

Before anyone called me a skater — before coaches, classes, drills, and medals — there was only a small boy standing on one foot in the centre of the living room floor, attempting to balance like the heroes he'd read about in books and seen on television. His love for skating was already budding, a passion shaping his future.

When I was a little child, my school requested that we pick a "sport of choice." My parents were completing the form—one of those large admission forms where every box appears to be important. And even though I couldn't even hold a pencil properly, they said to me, "Aarush, what sport do you want to try?"

The school had alternatives: football, swimming, table tennis, taekwondo, and basketball. But I chose skating. There was no hesitation, no uncertainty, just a firm, cheerful, little voice uttering that one, a voice that was already determined and committed to the path it had chosen.

Back in those days, the whole house was a skating rink. The soft silk rug in the living room was smooth enough for spins (even though I used to fall most of the time). The bed was ideal for standing on one leg (soft landings guaranteed). Even the corridor would become an outside stage if you leaned your head and dreamed just right. I'd lift my leg, arms raised, sometimes smashing into a pillow or a chair. Then again. And once more. I'd study the way skaters on television skated and try to imitate them with utmost seriousness. I had imagination — enough to transport me into a world of grace and freedom.

And Mumma?

She always watched, never made a big deal about it, never interrupted, but she noticed everything.

As I wobble like a confused flamingo, I'd catch her smiling from the corner of my eye as she poured her tea. Sometimes, she'd scoop me up with one arm — still holding her cup in the other — and say, "My little skater is flying again." Her joy was palpable, filling the room with warmth and happiness.

Can you picture it? One arm around a wobbly giggling kid, the other hand smoothly pouring hot tea. Mumma made it all so easy. She was stable, even when I was not. That's where I first discovered proper balance—physically and in life.

Skating came to me in glimpses —

Through colouring book pages with figures in helmets and skates. Through bedtime stories, Mumma read, where someone always soared. In flashes on the news, when Papa changed channels, I saw athletes run like the wind. I didn't know their names. But I knew I wanted to experience what they did. So, I began practising. Small efforts, daily. One up on a leg. Arms outstretched. Falling on my back and laughing. Sometimes, I cried. But I always tried again. I didn't realize I was training. I was merely playing, dreaming, and moving. The essence of my journey was the joy of learning through play, discovering new skills, and pushing my limits. And then, one day, without much ado, Mumma signed me up for skating lessons.

She didn't tell me, "Now you have to take this seriously."

She gave me this little pair of skates and said, "Let's go."

That was when I had my first coach. That's when I learned all about posture, push, stop, bend, and glide. That's when I realized all those carpet falls had already taught me something important.

They showed me that balance isn't something you learn. It's something you feel. And it starts in the home. On plush carpets. On mattresses. In the arms of a mother who holds you with one hand and pours tea with another — steady and calm as can be — like she already knows you'll make it.

Entry 9: From Belief to Blueprint

There's a moment when a hobby turns into a decision. Not just in your heart — but in your home.

Skating had already taken over my thoughts, routines, and off-days. I was eating better, sleeping with routines playing in my head, and missing the rink like it was a best friend I hadn't seen in days. My family could see it before I could say it. So one evening, after dinner, we talked.

It wasn't deliberate. There was no "we must have a seat and talk about your future" type of thing. There were just the four of us in the dining room—Papa, Mumma, Bhaiya, and me—plates moved to the sides, steam wafting up from freshly poured tea.

Papa began it in his characteristic, even, reflective manner. "Is this not just a phase?" he asked, looking directly at me. "Are you ready to commit to skating and all the things that go along with it?" He didn't pose it as a challenge. It wasn't a test. It was an offer to be truthful with myself.

I didn't respond right away. I glanced down at my hands, followed the rim of my cup of hot chocolate with marshmallows, and nodded. Slowly. As if I were committing to something holy. Something true.

Mumma didn't charge in. She just looked at me for a moment with that quiet, soft face she always wears when something counts. Then she asked softly, "Tell us why, Aarush. Not why you like it — we know that. Why does it feel like more?" And I told them. How it wasn't fun anymore. How I missed it when I wasn't skating. How it had become like me.

"I don't just like skating," I said in a low voice, my eyes searching for understanding in my family's faces. Mumma's eyes softened, Papa's brows furrowed in concern, but there was also a glint of pride in his eyes.

"I feel like it's choosing me too."

Mumma smiled and reached across to grab my hand. "Then we do it properly," she said. "And we do it together." That's when the honest conversations started. We discussed the sacrifices, the commitment, and the challenges. But we also talked about the joy, the victories, the shared moments of triumph. It was a dialogue that brought us closer, that made us a team. Papa switched modes — Practical Papa mode but with a hint of adaptability. "Okay," he said, reaching for his phone. Let's look at your schedule. We'll need to build in time for rest, schoolwork, and travel, and we'll need to talk about costs—gear, training, and competitions." Mumma nodded. "And food. If you're serious, your body has to be taken care of. No more skipping water. And enough sleep — that's non-negotiable." And then, like always, Archit Bhaiya leaned back in his chair and smirked. "Well, if skating is your life now," he said, "I'm making you a playlist. And I'll help with science while you stretch your calves. I'm officially your cool assistant."

We all laughed — the good kind of laughter, where everyone is relaxed, even while talking about serious things. But in between the jokes, they were all honest with me. "There are going to be bad days," Papa said. "You'll wonder why you did this. You'll be tired. Maybe even falling behind in school. But we'll cope — as long as you're truthful with us and with yourself." "And we'll ask you why you began," Mumma said, staring directly at me. Bhaiya raised his hand like a student in school. "And I'll remind you that you still owe me chocolate if you win your next competition." It wasn't pressure. It was preparation — firm and full of love.

After I had gone to bed that evening, I found out later that Mumma had whispered a phone call to my grandparents. Their support and blessings were crucial in this journey. She always spoke to them when something big was happening. I imagined her soft voice on the phone, explaining the decision, telling them about the long conversation, the new training plan, and the dreams we'd spoken aloud. They listened, like they always do. Then Nana, in his calm and grounding tone, said something simple: "If this brings him closer to who he's meant to be, it's worth every effort."

It wasn't just about training now. It was about faith. From that evening on, everything shifted. Practice sessions were timed around study sessions. We began monitoring nutrition. Family outings were plotted with competition dates. Bhaiya started taking me through YouTube clips of international figure skaters and slow-motion replays of flawless landings. Even our refrigerator changed—more fruits, more protein, less chips (to my silent dismay). This shift in our family dynamics was not just about accommodating my new passion but about everyone actively participating in my journey. And no one ever made me feel like it was a burden. They made it feel like a mission together. One that we were on together.

If you ask me when things got serious with skating, I won't cite a competition.I'll reference that dinner table — and that late-night call. Because that night, I didn't decide to skate.

We all decided.

My grandparents- The roots that hold me steady

Entry 10: More Than Just Skates

At first, skating was something I did. It was like a painting, playing catch with my brother or making random animal sounds to make Mumma laugh. It was fun, exciting, tricky, and mostly messy. But I loved it, and that felt like enough.

Suddenly, the fun I had with skating took on a new dimension. Something changed — not in one dramatic flash, but gradually, like water pouring into a glass. Without noticing it, I moved from liking skating to requiring it.

Upon waking from a good night's sleep, my thoughts focused less on upcoming tasks and more on the uncertainties of skating. Reviewing my routines before bed became a calming ritual, like a meditative lullaby. On days off from practice, I felt incomplete, as if part of my day was missing. My feet itched to move, my muscles craved the stretch, and my mind yearned for the serene focus that skating provided.

I felt skating was like a shadow — always with me. Not the scary kind. The kind that stays close, even when the lights are gone. Even in darkness, it stayed — just a feeling at my back, reminding me that this was part of me now. Sometimes, I'd be eating lunch, and suddenly, I'd start tapping my fingers in the rhythm of my new routine. Or I'd stand up and absentmindedly try balancing on one foot while brushing my teeth. I was breathing, dreaming, eating, and skating. And the weird part? I liked it. The obsession I felt serene. As if it made me more me. But it wasn't all smiles and twirls. As the dream intensified, so did the pressure. After a few wins at the competition, my confidence was in full bloom — a new kind of smile resided on my face. One that whispered, "Perhaps I can actually do this."

But with that confidence came something else as well.

Doubt.

Not the epic, dramatic, throw-in-the-towel sort.

The tiny, whispery sort.

"Can I do this?"

"What if I flop in front of everyone?"

"What if I can't juggle this with school, studies, and life?"

There were days when I'd look at my homework and skates and feel torn. I didn't want to choose. I wanted both. I wanted to be a skater, a bright student, a good son, and a normal kid who could hang out with friends without worrying about warm-ups, routines, or injuries.

Some nights, I left practice utterly drained, legs burning, and questioning myself: Is this passion, or am I pushing myself too hard? And then, the morning after, I'd wake up before everyone else, buckling my laces tighter than ever. That was my cue.

Skating wasn't merely something I enjoyed. I couldn't release it —even on bad days, despite the questions and the exhaustion. It offered me something no other aspect of my life ever did—a rhythm, a rush, a reason. And as I took things more seriously, so did my questions. That's when my older brother became a whole new type of support system. I'd sit next to him and plead, "Can you find something about skating today? Please? Can I see pictures?" And he always obliged. He'd open up pages with skaters—roller skaters, figure skaters, athletes in mid-spin, mid-jump, mid-magic—and read me the most awesome facts. But he didn't just read them aloud. He brought them to life.

He made the complicated simple — the history of figure skating, the development of roller sports, stories of world champions who skated in the snowstorm or after getting hurt. He shared the earliest skates ever constructed, the world's youngest world champions, the international rinks and their bizarre ice customs. It wasn't informative only. It was entertaining. It was as if I was being taught by someone who understood precisely how my mind functioned. And the best part? He never made my interest feel like it was too much. He stoked it. He made me believe that the world of skating wasn't far off — it was at hand, right there, on our television, in our living room, close enough to touch. That's when I understood: Skating was no longer a pastime. It was everything. It had become the one thing I couldn't quit loving — even when it became difficult. The thing I missed when I wasn't doing it. The thing I discussed, inquired about and sought out. It was the thing that made me feel small and powerful simultaneously. Skating had turned into something more than something I did. Skating had evolved from something I did to something I was becoming.

Entry 11: Outgrowing Gold

Winning felt like flying.

At an age when most kids were still figuring out what they liked, I was already standing on podiums, medals clinking around my neck, my name echoing through loudspeakers. Roller skating felt like magic under my feet. I loved the speed, spins, and thrill of getting it right. I was young, but skating made me feel braver and sharper — like I had found my place before anyone had asked me to.

Every competition, every medal, every cheer made the world my own. I wasn't skating – I was flying. School friends called me "the skater," and coaches started discussing my "potential." Our wall gradually disappeared under certificates and medals in our living room at home. And I thought, perhaps this is it — maybe I've found my forever. But I didn't realize that a turning point was waiting for me in secret, behind all the bright lights and applause.

One afternoon, after practice, my roller skating coach took me aside. His tone was soft, but his words changed everything:

"Aarush, you've outgrown this." I didn't get it at first. But then he told me. I had achieved nearly all that roller skating had to give — at least here, in Delhi and India. There were no high-tech facilities or national setups to propel roller skaters onward. My coach, who had shown me to trust the beat of my wheels, now thought I was mentally, physically, and technically prepared to jump into something completely different.

"It's time you go to ice skating," he told me.

My world spun. Ice skating? I'd watched that on YouTube — in Olympic stadiums, not Gurgaon. I'd never even been on ice.

But something within me — a soft but stern voice — urged: Try.

And that's when we discovered it—the only mall with an ice rink anywhere near us: Ambience Mall, Gurgaon. It's not a professional academy—it's a mall with a single rink. It wasn't close—an hour away—when traffic was good. That meant two hours of travelling each time I needed to train, but if I was going to pursue this new dream, I had no other option.

And this is where Mumma and Suraj Bhaiya became the wind beneath my skates.

Four times a week — yes, four — they accompanied me to that rink. They accommodated their own lives to mine, traffic, delays, tiredness, routines, group assignments, projects, weekly tests — complaining, not once, so I could get in one more hour on the ice.

I recall sitting in the mall on those cold benches, wearing a scarf, holding her bag, and waiting patiently for my turn to be over. Suraj Bhaiya was reading stories about skating between turns, tightening my laces, and recording my performances so I could analyze them later. It wasn't glamorous, easy, or even comfortable. It was love — the loud, inconvenient, powerful kind.

But ice skating wasn't a surface adjustment. It was a whole new language. I didn't know then how different it would be. The angles on ice are smaller, like navigating a maze of frozen pathways. Skates consist of a single thin blade, a delicate instrument of balance, rather than four wide wheels, so your centre of balance changes entirely. In roller skating, I learned to push with power and control through friction. Friction is the foe on ice — gliding, carving, and cutting through cold air is all about it. You can't stop in the same manner. You can't even fall in the same way.

Even my stance had to be retrained. The body is more inclined forward on ice. The arms must be lighter, and the knees must yield more. The edges you glide on—the inside and outside—are foreign at first. My footwork, which used to make audiences applaud, now causes me to stumble. Over and over.

It was like beginning at level zero. All of the techniques I had learned had to be forgotten and relearned. My muscles, accustomed to the push-pull of rubber wheels, shrieked in protest on the slippery surface. My core had to improve, my legs more powerful, and my mind more composed. Roller made me challenging. Ice was going to make me precise.

That was when Coach J. S. Sahney came into my life. The first time I met him, he didn't have much to smile about. But he observed me — not sceptically, but hopefully. He saw I had a lot to learn, and he wouldn't tell me otherwise.

Ice skating was a whole new world. It was cold, slippery, and unpredictable. I fell, stumbled, and flailed in all directions. Everything I had learned on wheels seemed distant and irrelevant. I had to start from scratch with bruises, sore muscles, and a renewed determination.

But with each crash, I got back up again. Because each commuting hour and every bit of sweat my family had put into this aspiration mattered. I couldn't squander it.

Every day, I lost my fear of the ice. I started gliding. I started believing. And one day, I didn't fall. I soared.

That was when I realized I was no longer transitioning. I had arrived.

Roller skating wasn't replaced by ice skating. It was the next chapter. A colder and harder one. But also — a clearer instalment. With aspirations that reached farther than I ever imagined I could.

Because in the end, it wasn't just the blades, rink, or coaching.

It was the sacrifices behind the scenes.

It was love — pushing me forward, every frozen step of the way.

Entry 12: When Dreams Found a Face

When I first began skating, I didn't have any idols.

None.

I did not wake up wanting to be like somebody. I was not watching highlight reels or plastering posters on the wall. I was too young for all that — too busy with the wonder of simply moving, falling, flying, and laughing.

The rink, then, was not a stage. It was a big playground with sparkle at my feet. Skating, for me, was a source of pure joy. It was a feeling that made my heart beat faster in the best possible way, a sensation that I couldn't get enough of. And that was enough. I didn't know what a "role model" was or what a world record was. I just knew that the world became a different and happier place when I was wearing the wheels. It was pure, personal, and mine.

Even when I took my first classes and began attending regularly and doing drills and warm-ups, I never considered champions or medals. I was not skating to become somebody. I was skating because something in me needed to.

My family witnessed that passion. And as they always did, they did what they could to encourage it — subtle, loving, thoughtful gestures.

There was a period when I had some trouble with balance and flexibility. My coach recommended some off-ice exercises like breathing, stretching, and strengthening to support movement. We could have signed up for a class or located a program, but my family did something better. It joined in.

My family didn't just watch from the sidelines. Mumma laid out the yoga mats in the living room, Papa found the best YouTube tutorials, and even my usually laid-back older brother took on the role of' yoga master', turning each pose into a friendly competition.

And there we were — all four — wobbling and bending in unnatural angles, attempting to support our "vajrasana" and "tree pose" without falling over.

I can still hear Papa's grunts as he struggled through the planks, Mumma's attempts to maintain a straight face while secretly keeping an eye on my posture, and my brother's dramatic fall over the couch. Laughter often overtook our stretching, but the results were undeniable. My spine strengthened, my legs steadied, and my focus sharpened.

And beyond that , it brought us closer still.

Skating was my dream, but memories like these reminded me that my dream had a team—a team that appeared on yoga mats, in grocery store aisles (scanning for calcium-filled foods), at dinner tables, and beside the rink.

But even after discovering that spark of inspiration, transitioning to ice skating was one of the hardest things I've ever done.

I began roller skating when I was only four and a half. Wheels were familiar, and the floor was home. Ice was like another planet—colder, more complex, and much less tolerant. Every step felt unbalanced, and every fall was more difficult. I had to relearn posture, rhythm, and even how to stop. It was infuriating, draining, and, in some moments, downright terrifying.

But I did not give up.

Gradually, the wobbles stabilized into glides. I started believing in the ice under me. And then, at 11, something magical happened — I won my first National Gold Medal in ice skating. Then, another. Two-time National Champion. For India.

That changed everything.

The confidence I possessed on wheels began to return; but this time, on blades. The fear became fuel. I started not just to enjoy the ice but to love it. I knew, with absolute certainty, this is where my future lies.

I have never looked back since.

I've completely stopped competing in roller skating. My heart and training are fully committed to ice now. It's not just a sport anymore. It's my path, my purpose.

I've been honoured to represent India in international events, including the Thailand Trophy and the Asian Open. Skating under the national flag and sharing the rink with athletes from across the globe is surreal, humbling, and powerful.

And each time I skate, I'm carrying my dream and all those who believed in it, along with me.

But idols? That thought hadn't come yet. That came way later.

I recall it well, one evening — though it was nothing more than a fleeting instant on television.

Papa was channel-surfing after dinner. I was reclined on the floor, half-inattentive, when he paused. The television was displaying a ribbon of glinting white — an ice rink. A skater in a glittering blue costume stood motionless in the centre.

Then, the music began.

And he moved.

The room fell silent. Not because anyone told us to be quiet but because something about how he skated asked for silence. Mumma paused with her cup of tea halfway to her lips. Papa didn’t change the channel. I sat up without thinking.

He twirled. He jumped. He landed as lightly as a feather.

"Who is that?" I breathed.

"Yuzuru Hanyu," Papa said. " He is from Japan. He is one of the best figure skaters I have seen."

I stared without flinching. Until the very end beat. Until he bowed.

And even then, I couldn't budge.

Something profound had shifted. Not in the world around me but deep within.

That night, I didn't just go to bed wondering about skating.

I drifted off, attempting to recall his steps, not to mimic but to be inspired.

Yuzuru Hanyu didn't begin my dream. Yuzuru Hanyu didn't just give my dream a face; but he gave it a soul.

Before him, I was an enthusiastic ice skater, but after witnessing his performance, I became a skater with a clear purpose.

And that is what idols truly are.

They do not give you wings.

They remind you that you already possess them, and teach you to fly.

Behind every great skater is a phenomenal coach — With our respected coach – a true guiding force behind my journey on the ice .Grateful for his constant support and mentorship.

Entry 13: Training, Tears, and Timetables

Skating had always felt like freedom to me. But freedom, I soon learned, comes at a cost — especially when you want to take it seriously. The move from casual skating to structured, professional training was a shift for me and my entire family. Before my first professional session, there was a *storm of planning* behind the scenes. While I was still spinning on our living room carpet, dreaming of gliding better, my parents were *making things happen.*

It began with a decision: *Aarush is serious. We need to find him the proper guidance.* And that's where the work started.

Mumma and Papa did not simply Google "Best skating coach nearby." They went into full detective mode. They approached other parents at the rink, friends of friends, neighbours, and distant relatives whose children had once skated. They checked out training centres in Delhi, jotting down notes like reporters on the coaches, their method, qualifications, safety norms, charges, how many children per batch, and how much individual attention each child would receive.

They weren't searching for a coach. They were searching for a suitable coach to look beyond technique and nurture a young kid rather than burn him out. Papa phoned one academy six times a week to learn how the two levels of coaching differed. Mumma listened to hour-long discussions with parents who offered candid insights into the highs and lows of specific locations. And once they settled on a coach they were pleased with, that wasn't it yet. They needed to meet my school principal.

Being a professional skater doesn't mean taking an extra class or two. It means giving up school time for morning practice sessions, travel days to competitions, and recovery from long tournaments. So, Mumma emailed and asked for a meeting.

They entered that school office not only as parents but also as my advocates. Mumma sat across from the Principal—a stern, tall woman. Mumma underlined my journey and how this wasn't just a passing phase. She shared videos, spoke about progress, and noted my training hours. She inquired, politely and hopefully, if the school could be accommodating. If they could permit me to miss classes now and then for competitions or grant me a lighter homework load during peak training sessions. Mumma had a folder full of my progress photos, report cards, and practice videos on her phone, which she shared with our Principal. In this way, Ma'am got a bird's eye view of the whole picture. She described how professional skating involved early-morning practice, frequent travel, mental preparation, and rest. She inquired if there could be space — a bit of flexibility on time, tolerance if assignments were a day behind, and understanding when the road ahead was unfamiliar. She wasn't demanding special privilege; she was asking for understanding.

My father said, "Ma'am, this is not a passing interest for Aarush. It's a growing discipline. And we're not asking to take him away from school, but to help him balance both."

There was a pause. The Principal leaned back and smiled. "You're raising a child with a dream," she said. "We will stand by him. Just keep us informed. Let's go through this step by step." Mumma and Papa smiled, thanked her, and left quietly.

I wasn't present, but I later learned about it—not in the way she told me in the form of a report, but because I happened to overhear her speaking to Papa in the kitchen, her voice low but slightly trembling, as if someone who had held their breath all day. Still, nothing fell into place. It took repeated check-ins, reminders, and parent-teacher conferences that became mini-strategy sessions on how I would do schoolwork without giving up on my dream.

Later that night, I noticed something. She sat on the edge of her bed, still in her work kurta, hair tied back, shoulders slightly hunched. She wasn't crying. But her eyes were glassy. Not sad — just tired. I quietly walked over, put my head on her lap, and said nothing. She touched my head and whispered, "We'll do this. One practice at a time." That minute made it seem real, more than any spin I had made. Because then I knew what it cost — not only for me but for all of us.

At home, it meant restructuring life. My parents constructed my day like a puzzle — skating, school, rest, study, nutrition. Mumma packed energy bars in her bag like they were gold. Papa rearranged his appointments to take me to morning sessions when necessary. They worked calendar dates like a war operation — even one overscheduled time slot could ruin everything. And here's the amazing part: I hardly ever saw them complain. They were exhausted. Stretched thin. But never absent. All I had to do was skate. They handled everything else. So, while I was out there learning to spin tighter, jump higher, and pay attention, they performed a different balancing act behind the scenes.

To speak my heart out, despite my academic performance being appreciated — certificates, trophies, even a few school assembly mentions — there was still silence around my achievements in skating. No bulletin board displays for medals won at state-level competitions or announcements when I returned from a podium finish. Sports, unless part of the school curriculum, remained on the sidelines. But Mumma and Papa didn't stop. They continued to advocate, gently but persistently, for equal recognition. Not just for me but for every child chasing excellence outside the classroom. "If academics deserve applause," Mumma once said during a parent-teacher meeting, "then so does discipline, perseverance, and success in any field." They weren't asking for banners or glory, just acknowledgement that dreams come in more forms than test scores.

During those days of counterbalancing training and academics, I often wondered if my efforts were seen outside the rink. While school celebrated academic achievements with certificates and statements, sports usually remained an afterthought. But Mumma and Papa's quiet hard work didn't go unnoticed. At one point, my photo and story were included in my school, DPS Vasant Kunj's magazine titled "DIPSVISION"—a recognition that carried tremendous meaning. Among the pages, there it was—a photo of me, poised at the rink, a big smile on my face, my upper body draped in the vibrant folds of the Indian flag. The photograph wasn't just a snapshot; it was a story. The fabric billowed around me like a protective cloak, whispering tales of resilience and pride. My skates sparkled under the smooth rink lights, and my face and posture said everything—shoulders strong, spine straight, head held high as if still listening to the distant echoes of cheering and clapping.

It was more than just a photo of a boy skating. It was a portrayal of a young idealist bearing the dreams of a family, a community, and a nation in addition to his own. It was movement captured in stillness—the quiet power of a child turning ambition into action wrapped not just in the tricolour but in the love and support of everyone who believed in him.

In another such episode of my life, Mumma explained how the school magazine, which was published during the celebrations for the school's 30th anniversary, highlighted students' accomplishments outside of the classroom, including mine. A special section called "Striding Through the Annals of Excellence, 1994–2004," which highlighted student achievements, featured my photo and story. It was my accomplishment, my picture, standing tall among the best; it wasn't just a mention.

Classmates, seniors and juniors would exclaim, "Hey, Aarush, your picture is here!" when they saw the magazine. It was a proud moment for both my family and me. Papa even made a joke about how my peers could now see my journey in print rather than just cheering at competitions.

That little mention in the school publication served as a reminder that triumphs can take many different forms and that any honour, no matter how small, can encourage a young person's ambitions. It was satisfaction in action—gentle but determined, noiseless but resonant.

I realised that professional training didn't just push me—it pushed us. And what kept me going through the most demanding, earliest stages wasn't my strength.

It was theirs.

Entry 14: The Dreams Get Bigger

My initial roller skating competitions were all about the adrenaline.

I wasn't concerned with rankings or the future. I just wanted to get on the rink, hear my name called out, and feel the crowd's buzz. I skated in all sorts of events — district meets, state championships, national tournaments — and it was like surfing on a golden wave for a time.

I won gold in most competitions I participated in.

We travelled everywhere, sometimes on our motorcycle, with skates strapped to the side, bags packed tightly, and routes half-planned. Some places were familiar, others completely new. We'd reach small towns between fields or cities we'd only seen on maps. It wasn't always comfortable. But it was always worth it.

The excitement of a new rink, the nervous hush before a performance, the moment my music would start, the world would shrink to just me and the ice (or floor)—memories I'll never forget.

But here's the thing: I didn't always win.

There were days I fell, days when my balance played hide-and-seek, and my medals slipped away. And those moments hurt. But they taught me something significant—if I wanted to stay in this long term, something had to change.

As I mentioned earlier, I had been skating enthusiastically until now. But now, I was skating with intent. By this time, my confidence gradually increased since the switch from roller to ice; what had initially felt strange had become familiar. Fighting for two National Gold Medals in ice skating was a turning point for the medals themselves and for what they represented: that I belonged here, pursuing something more prominent. The more I became enthralled with the sport — the precision it required, the quiet before a routine, the raw power in every motion — the more I saw that this wasn't something I did; it was something I was. It was who I was turning into. That certainty gave me something more significant than any medal I'd ever received: the Olympic dream. It began as a whisper, but with every stroke of the blade, each early morning, each breath on the ice, it grew louder.

My dream of Olympic glory started when I skated in the Thailand Open and the Asian Open Figure Skating Trophy tournaments. The former allows skaters worldwide to compete and obtain international experience by offering single skating disciplines at the Basic Novice, Intermediate Novice, Advanced Novice, Junior, and Senior levels. Top talent from across the continents competes in the latter, a prestigious annual competition approved by the Asian Skating Union. It features novice, junior, and senior levels of ice dancing, pair skating, and men's and women's singles.

As I represented India on these occasions, I realised that practice wasn't enough. I needed to perform—to walk with control, maturity, and poise—to "arrive" in front of the audience like a skater who was supposed to be there, not just one who happened to show up. That change of mind led me to study more about the global figure skating universe.

That is when I stumbled upon the Junior Grand Prix and Senior Grand Prix—the two largest competitive series in world figure skating, held under the International Skating Union (ISU) umbrella.

Here's what I learned:

- The Junior Grand Prix is for skaters under 19 (for singles) or under 21 (for pairs and ice dance). It's organized to give bright young skaters international experience. They earn points at each event, and the leading six in each discipline qualify for the Junior Grand Prix Final.

- The Senior Grand Prix is the elite tier — for the best skaters at the multinational level. There's no age limit. Like the junior version, skaters compete to earn points and reach the Grand Prix Final. This series began in 1992 and is where legends are made.

I scanned around and saw more than skaters. I saw teams—organized, focused, and supported, with uniforms, coaches, and synchronized training schedules. I also saw international skaters, visitors, guests, and teams gearing up for bigger arenas.

"This isn't just a sport," I thought. This is a transnational stage.

That was the first time I felt drawn to something bigger.

Not as a far-off dream but an ideal to work for, with integrity, commitment, and every ounce of energy I had.

I came to understand at the time that I couldn't remain where I was.

Not just physically. Mentally. Technically. Professionally.

Participation in these events is more than a milestone — it's a step onto the world stage. Competing alongside skaters from across the globe and hearing my name announced with the Indian flag beside it gave me a glimpse of what I was truly working toward. It reminded me how far I had come and how much farther I wanted to go. Those moments made the Dream of the Five Rings feel genuine and reachable.

This impacted more than just winning national medals or standing alone on a podium. It involved India stepping into global arenas where flags wave high, anthems resound, and international eyes observe every move. And I crave that. I aim to stand with the world's best and skate with intention, composure, and honour—not just for myself but for my nation.

That aspiration ignited a spark in me. I began to explore the journey that could lead me there — from the Junior Grand Prix to the Senior Circuit to the Olympics. I learned that this dream would require more than skill. It would need determination, self-control, and faith.

I long to hear "India" announced after my performance. I want to experience the quiet before my opening stance on international ice. I strive to symbolize something bigger than myself and do it with elegance, power, and spirit.

The journey is long. But every medal I've won, every defeat I've gained insights from, and every mile we drove to get to one more ice rink — they've all moulded my identity.

Now, I don't just aim to come out on top.

I want to belong.

To make my mark.

To carry India with me — blade by blade, breath by breath — onto the world stage.

Entry 15: Between School Bells and Ice Falls

Most people think skating is all sparkle and spotlight. They see the final performance — the jump, the spin, the smile at the end. What they don't see is everything that happens before the music starts. And honestly? That's where the real story is.

My mornings are not like most other schoolkids'. While many are still sleeping or slowly getting ready for school, my day starts before sunrise. I wake up very early — not because I like it, but because I must. There's no time to relax. I quickly eat breakfast, stretch, and get ready to leave.

I'm going to school after a lightning-fast breakfast and a lightning-fast stretch. On the outside, I'm sitting in my classroom like everyone else. But on the inside? My mind's racing through timetables. "Do I have time to get that science worksheet done before practice? Did I bring my rink gear? Can I study chapters tonight after training? " It's like a tightrope walk — except the rope is on fire, and I'm carrying textbooks in one hand and skates in the other.

And then there is travelling. My training venue is far from home, draining me of time and energy on most occasions.

And the training? It's not just gliding in circles. There's off-ice practice, exhausting, sweaty, muscle-burning work that doesn't even touch the ice. We practice jumps without skates. Spins without blades. And when I finally get the skates on? I have to repeat it all over again, but better. My legs hurt. My back cramps. There are days when I feel like I am being pulled from all sides.

And what about the skates? They're not gentle slippers. They bite. I return home with cuts, bruises, blisters, and toes that are swollen. When I take off my socks, I see the impressions — deep red traces of each minute I spent in the rink. But for some reason, those impressions no longer frighten me. They push me forward.

The practice does not end after the day. I have exams, homework, tuition classes to attend, and projects. I eat while I revise and sleep while I do mathematics. Some evenings, I'm so fatigued that I could sleep standing up. And still, I go on.

Because I know this life is not easy. It's not supposed to be.

People who reach for the stars don't receive smooth roads. They receive bumpy ones, full of challenges, sacrifices, and people telling you it's too complicated.

I miss birthday parties, lazy afternoons, and just sitting and doing nothing. But I don't regret missing those things. When you choose something extraordinary, you must let go of ordinary comforts. I chose this life—not because it's easy, but because it matters to me. Sometimes, I wonder what life would be like without this dream. Then I recall: I wouldn't exchange this existence for anything.

While others may follow a straight path, I carve mine with willpower, hard work, and faith. And each day, with each fall and every push, I'm building something that no one can take from me. This is not merely a day in motion. It's a life in the making.

So the next time you notice someone twirling around the ice, receiving a medal, or standing erect on a podium — stop. Take a closer look. Behind that picture is a hill of sacrifices, late nights, sore muscles, and silent struggles no one applauds for.

Everyone desires the glory. But not everyone will bear the burden it takes to arrive there. And if you ever wonder whether the pain, the pressure, and the push are worth it — ask yourself this:

Do you want an everyday life or a life that makes you feel truly alive?

Dreams don't just ask for your talent; they ask for everything. And I've decided to give it.

With Mr. Amitabh Sharma, *President, Ice Skating Association of India* (right)— proud moment receiving the trophy at the 18th National Speed and Figure Skating Championship 2023, Gurugram, India

Entry 16: Restart > Quit

There are days when everything feels like too much.

It's not just tiring but truly overwhelming.

No matter how hard you try, nothing works.

It's like your brain is heavy, your body has already given up, and your heart is just trying to hang on.

I've had those days. And I remember one in particular like it just happened yesterday.

It began like any other school day. But I had slept only five hours the previous night, catching up on completing a Science project, studying for an exam, and packing my training equipment. My back was stiff from stretching the night before. I yawned throughout the first period and left a notebook behind in the second, and by lunchtime, I could already sense the headache coming on.

We left for practice right after school. The drive to Gurgaon took an hour, and the traffic felt extra slow that day. I remember staring out the window, my eyelids heavy, my mind saying, "Do you have anything left to give today?"

But I still put on my skates.

I still warmed up.

And then, I couldn't do anything right. My spin tilted strangely, and I landed late. My arms were inflexible, and my head was foggy. My coach called twice to fix the same issue. I behaved as if I had understood his instructions. But to be honest, I had no clue what he meant to explain. I felt like all my energy had been pumped out of me.

After the session, I didn't want to untie my skates when I finally sat down.

I was depressed, as if my body had lied to me and my efforts were no longer significant. The worst part? I wanted to cry. But I couldn't even gather the energy for tears.

We drove back in silence. I didn't want to talk. I just leaned my head against the window and closed my eyes.

Later that day, I sat alone by my bedroom window and saw a tiny, bright blue bird. It circled back and forth, attempting to build a nest. It kept coming back, bringing more twigs and leaves, even though the wind kept blowing away its work. I spent some time watching it. It persisted, remained calm, and continued to build. Something inside me whispered, "If that bird isn't quitting, why should I?" during that brief, silent moment.

A little later, Mumma and Papa walked in. She didn't say much at first but understood what I was feeling. Gently, Mumma said, "It's okay to talk about giving up if that's how you feel. But before you decide, think about how far you've come."

Papa nodded and added, "Quitting is the easy part. Starting over, that's tough. But haven't you faced tougher things before—and made it through?"

They were right. I had.

There's something no one prepares you for — the amount of pain that comes with this sport. Skating is highly technical in addition to being artistic. You fall hard if you make even a tiny mistake in timing or angle. You suffer harm. You sustain an injury. On some days, after removing my socks, I discovered new cuts around my toes from the strain of skating for hours on end. Blisters. Bruises. Bleeding. I still had to stretch, smile, and return to the rink afterwards.

With my legs stretched on a comfortable mattress, I reflect on my uncountable training hours. The birthdays I've missed. The friends I've waved goodbye to as they ran out to play. The moments I've said no to fun, to say yes to this dream. It's a lot. It's everything. And that's exactly why I can't walk away now.

~

The next day, the pain in my feet was still there. The bruises hadn't disappeared. But I laced up anyway. I was in the car when Suraj Bhiaya played the radio. The RJ was talking about Indian athletes. After three songs and a short break, he came back to talk about Mary Kom, the legendary boxer from Manipur, who trained in harsh conditions, faced judgment, and still became an Olympic medalist, not once, but again and again. She once said, "I was not born to give up." These words stayed with me, and I said, "And neither was I."

As a young child with so much happening in life, I sometimes envy the normal life others around me continue to live. But then I think about my family. Mumma travels with me for hours, and Papa always listens, even when I say nothing. Archit Bhiaya cheers me on like I've already won. Suraj Bhaiya knows every routine is his own. My grandparents whisper my name with every prayer bead. They're all still showing up — for me. So if they're not quitting, how can I? Discontinuing would mean giving up not just on myself — but on all of us.

This isn't just my dream anymore. We're all building it together, like that bird, one twig at a time. And someday, that nest will be complete. And when it is, I'll take flight.

Entry 17: Pain Has a Memory

During my summer vacation, there was this one day at practice when I believed I could endure the pain.

At first, it was only a minor ache close to my ankle. "Ignore it," I told myself. I was preparing for a previously performed jump combination but landed incorrectly in the middle of the spin. Like lightning, a sharp pain shot through my foot. I skid my blade. My knees buckled. And I fell to the ice. There was silence on the rink. Only my breath echoed inside my helmet, no music or applause.

Coach came skating over. "Did you listen to your body before this happened?" he asked, crouching beside me.

I was at a loss for words.

"Your body can take a lot," he said as he slowly helped me. "It's not a machine, though. If you want to skate for many years, you must treat it like a teammate rather than a tool." Given Coach's instructions, I was forced to take a few days off, not due to my laziness but because I realized for the first time that taking a break is not a sign of weakness. It's a sign of getting ready.

Learning that my vacation had begun, Nani came over to stay with us. Delhi summers are no joke. The heat feels like it's crawling into your skin, and even the fan sounds tired. That day, I felt drained—not just from training but from everything. My ankle was still hurting, and I couldn't stop thinking about how behind I was falling.

Nani, utterly unbothered by the weather, was making nimbu paani, her go-to solution for heat, tiredness, and life problems. I watched her slice a lemon and squeeze it over the glass.

And then she said something I didn't expect.

"Zyaada zor doge toh nimbu aur nimbu pani, dono bahut teetey ho jayengey," she muttered, laughing. *"If you press too hard, try to extract too much juice from the lemon; it will turn bitter, ruining the lemonade."* And I just stood there, thinking — Skating is like that lemon.

If you don't push yourself, you won't get much out of it. But if you push too hard, too fast, you burn out. You hurt yourself. It spills out and leaves a mess. The trick, just like Nani's lemon, is in the pressure. Not too soft. Not too harsh. Just right. That's what I've started learning — slowly, the hard way. I want to find balance in my routines, mindset, and how I train and rest.

When to fight. When to pause.

When to squeeze and when to breathe.

This sport and life are not about forcing every last dropout at once. It's about learning how to press and how to trust the flow.

Sometimes, the smallest lessons hide inside the simplest moments, like Nani making lemonade while the world outside was melting.

Gradually, I discovered little ways to get better during those revival days. When I got home, I discovered how to ice my foot. Despite not feeling like it, I stretched more. I began to pay attention to my breathing and learned how to stop my mind from racing when I was in pain.

Gradually, I discovered something amazing: I wasn't merely recovering my ankle. My brain was being trained. I told myself, "This is a setup for a better comeback," rather than, "This is a setback." Yes, skating is a physical activity. However, it's also very mental. When your body remembers the falls, your mind must remember the strength to keep fighting. Now, I don't panic when I feel pain. I pause. I ask myself, "Is this the kind of pain that grows me or the kind that warns me?" I've learned the difference. And that's how I keep moving.

One day, after I returned from that injury and landed the jump again — clean, fast, controlled — my coach applauded and said,

"Now *that's* how the body remembers and rewrites the story." It was one of the best compliments I've ever received.

So yes — the pain still comes. There are still cuts and blisters. My toes still get sore, and my socks come off with quiet winces. But now, every mark reminds me of pain and progress. And if I could say one thing to my body, it would be this:

"Dear legs, I know I push you hard. I know I ask you to fall and rise and fall again. But thank you for never giving up on me. I promise I'll keep listening. I promise I'll keep learning."

Because the body remembers. But the mind decides what it remembers. And I choose to remember the strength.

Entry 18: My Name. My Country. My Moment

Everything appeared and felt huge inside the Asian Open Figure Skating Trophy 2023 competition arena. It took place between August 16 and 19, 2023, at the IWIS International Training Center in Bangkok, Thailand. Organized by the Figure & Speed Skating Association of Thailand and sanctioned by the Asian Skating Union.

There were rows of flags, each brighter than the last, representing seventeen different countries, and the rink was wider than I had ever seen. During warm-ups, skaters from Korea, Kazakhstan, and Japan glided with ease. Their teams encircled them like a protective circle, their blades were sharp, and their uniforms were tailored. They did not appear uneasy. They appeared prepared. Some had entourages of coaches hovering nearby. Some stretched in perfect harmony. Others were absorbed in music, already skating programs in their minds. Their blades shone. Their expressions were unreadable. I had never seen such a thing before.

I stood aside, holding onto my gloves, with the buzz of nerves humming through my back. I wasn't scared — not really. But I knew. Knew about the gap. I knew that they had all been raised in rinks like this one. They likely didn't practice in malls. That their paths had been easier, glitzier, quicker.

And yet — I had arrived here. When the announcer's voice finally broke through the arena speakers, it sliced through everything else.

"Representing India... Aarush Tiwari." I had goosebumps. It wasn't just about hearing my name. It was the feeling of being there not just for myself and my family, but for my country. That one sentence made every sore muscle, every sacrificed holiday, and every hour in Gurgaon traffic worth it. Because it meant I wasn't just participating — I was representing.

The rink was enormous. Wider than anything I'd ever practised on. The lights appeared to pierce right into my soul. Officials lined the boards, along with coaches and cameras. There was a slight chill on the ice, yet my body was afire. Not with heat, but with the magnitude of what I would do. It wasn't fear. It wasn't panic. It was something more profound: honour. Because I wasn't skating for myself alone, I was skating for every individual who contributed to bringing me here: parents, grandparents, Suraj Bhaiya, Sahney Sir. I was skating for all the nights we skipped family dinner to practice, all the exams I prepared for in the car, and all the time my family waited while I practised behind the glass. I was skating for us.

I don't recall each jump and spin. What I recall is the crash of blades on ice. The silence before the music began. The way the audience didn't recognize me — but I knew I had something to prove. My program wasn't flawless. But it was true. And when it was over, I didn't wait to hear the scores. I closed my eyes for a moment. And smiled. Even Sahney Sir — who usually found something to critique, something to improve — said: "Good. You held your own." That was it. No long speeches. No gold star. Just that single word: Good. And coming from him, it felt better than any trophy.

When I went back to school, things had changed. When I missed birthday parties, the kids who used to roll their eyes now stopped me in the hallways. "Really, you appeared on television?" "Is that real ice, bro?" "Did they really call your name like that?" I said "Yes" to everything. Indeed, it brought about a change in me. Because that day, on unfamiliar ice in a foreign country, I didn't just compete. I didn't just perform. I became someone I didn't recognize, yet someone I had always been trying to become. Confident. Present. Capable.

Not because I won. But because I showed up — fully, vulnerably, proudly. The Asian Open 2023 gave me a new version of myself. And I took him home with me. That day, I didn't win a medal. But I didn't come back empty-handed either. Because what I carried home was more precious than gold — a belief that I belonged. Not because I was the best. But because I had become someone who dared to show up without the fanciest coaches, the glossiest costumes, or the cleanest landings, but with grit, with heart, and with everything I had.

That wasn't just my first international competition. It was my first real moment. The one that whispered: You're not a guest here anymore. This is your world, too.

And I believed it.

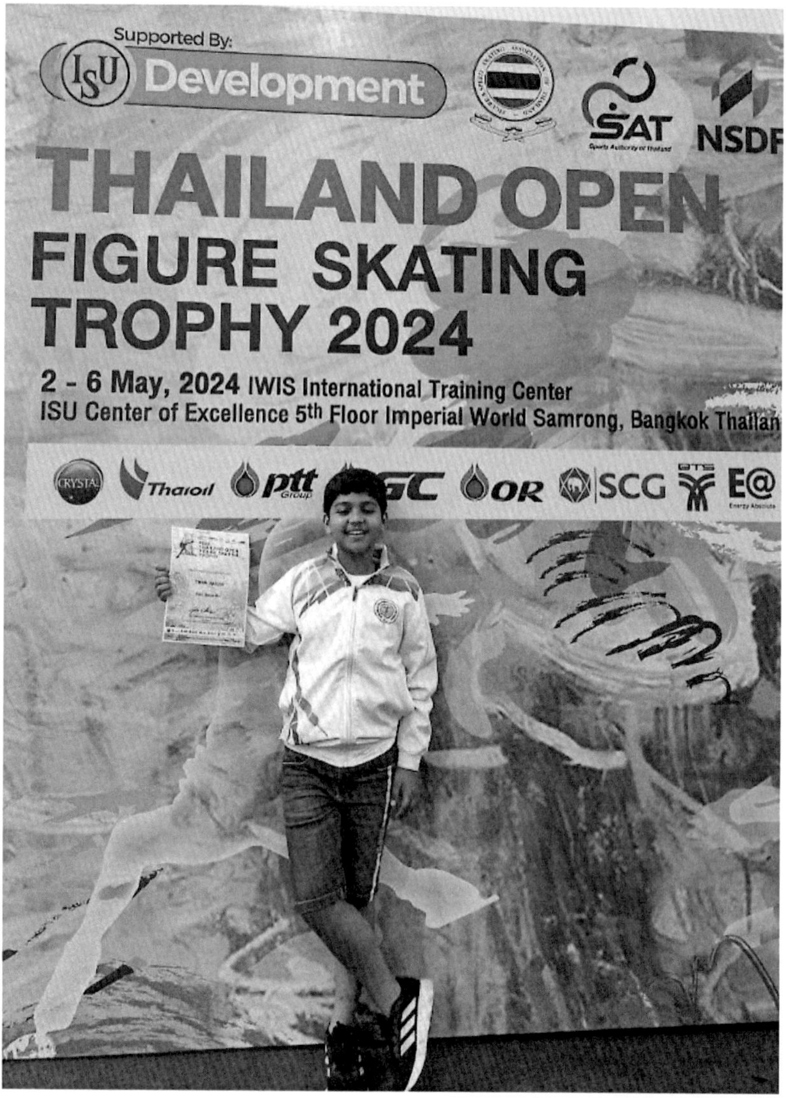

Representing India in the Asian Open Figure Skating Trophy 2023, Bangkok, Thailand. Standing tall with the Indian flag.

Entry 19: Pressure, Presence and the Pause

The 2024 Thailand Open Trophy was held in Bangkok from May 3rd to May 6th at the IWIS International Training Center — a sleek, silent place built for excellence. It wasn't about beaches, sticky rice, Pad Thai noodles, or the charm of travel. It was a pressure cooker disguised as an ice rink.

I came with hope in my heart and training in my bones. This was my second overseas competition. I had already represented India in the Asian Open, but this felt larger — not only in size but also in expectations. My program was crisp. My jumps were clean. We had worked hard and I felt ready. But belief isn't always enough when standing on unfamiliar ice, surrounded by unfamiliar silence.

I knew this was a different league when I walked into the practice rink. The players around me looked like they were meant to be there. They stretched in unison and worked in harmony with their coaches, their own physios, and video coaches. It was smooth, professional, and daunting. Nevertheless, I reminded myself I had worked for this place. I wasn't there as a participant. I was there as a competitor.

What amazed me, however, was how many of them were pretty much like me — driven, single-minded, and with their version of the same dream. We were from different origins and languages, but we had a hunger. I met a lot of skaters who, just like me, were skating nationally and internationally, and although we fought to say a lot — thanks to language differences — somehow we communicated. It was understood but not said: How do we improve? How do we do well? How far can we go with this sport?

There was this unspoken bond between us - a community of skaters who worked for years to perform well for three minutes on ice. But there was also a healthy spirit of competition, and that brought its share of pressure.

When my time arrived, I took to the rink with every fibre in my body. But something changed early on. My first jump was hasty. The timing was slightly off. I rebounded, but something was broken in my rhythm. The flow that had felt so natural in rehearsal now felt stiff. Mechanic. I gritted it out and saw the end of my routine — but I knew. I hadn't skated with my entire self.

No fall. No disaster. But no soaring either.

Backstage, everything was silent. My heart was beating louder than the crowd's. I did not move, did not want to remove my skates yet, and was not ready to meet anyone. Sahney Sir walked by and uttered only a single sentence: "You've trained harder than this." And he walked off. That stung more than I would have shouted. That evening in the hotel, I kept going over the routine in my head. Was it nervousness? Was it analysis paralysis? Was I out of rhythm or just overwhelmed? And the worst part: What would everybody think? But nobody ever made me feel like I'd failed. My mother didn't offer empty words of comfort. Instead, she reminded me, "It's okay to feel this way. But you can't let it stop you." Her words were a balm to my soul. That was enough.

Thailand wasn't a low point. It was a checkpoint, a reality check, a mirror. It reflected for me the difference between performing and performing with presence. It reflected for me that even when things go alright if they don't feel right inside, you still have work to do.

Back home, I did not brood. I worked harder, sharper, and cleaner. I studied tapes, sought corrections, and didn't wait for the next moment— I prepared for it. Because Thailand wasn't about a medal. It was about joining others on the same journey. It was about discovering how far I've come — and how far I still want to travel.

Entry 20: In Service of the Sport and the Flag

Before the spotlight hits, there's always silence.

Not outside — inside.It's the silence before music starts when my skates are on the ice, my arms are firm, and my mind is asking questions I can't always find the answers to. Will I get it right? Will I make my country proud?

Most individuals only observe the performance—the jumps, spins, choreography, and attire. However, they don't observe the silent battles that preceded it—the years of self-control, uncertainty, and intense concentration that construct a skater from the inside out.

I've trained since before everybody else wakes up. I've gone for my ice-skating training sessions on Diwali. I've missed summer vacations and winter breaks. I haven't played gully cricket with my dearest friends in ages. I don't even know when the last birthday party I stuck around for till the end was. Not because anybody made me leave things behind but because I chose something greater.

This is not sacrifice. This is my *duty*- my duty to the sport that shaped me, my duty to the country whose name I carry on my back whenever they call, *"Representing India: Aarush Tiwari."*

Even when no one was watching, I trained. Even when others celebrated, I practised. And even when it felt lonely, I reminded myself — this isn't a burden. This is a responsibility I'm honoured to carry. But I haven't done it alone. Mumma has waited for me to finish training in silence for hours while holding bags and drinking cold tea in waiting areas. Suraj Bhaiya never once expressed fatigue despite body aches from lengthy car trips—not a single grumble. I still can't adequately explain how my father, quiet and constant, has helped me realize this dream. I have witnessed the way he looks at me following a performance—not under compulsion but with conviction.

My coach, Sahney Sir, doesn't settle for mediocrity. He demands not just results, but relentless effort. He's the one who taught me that the goal isn't just to be good, but to be better every single day.

Yes, I've had to let go of things: friends, games, toys. But I don't see these as sacrifices. I see them as exchanges. I've traded one type of childhood for a purpose that extends beyond myself.

Yes, there is pressure, fear, critics, and comparisons, and days, I ask myself if I'm doing enough. But then I recall—I'm not doing it for claps alone. I'm doing it because I believe in the light that this sport casts and because I believe in the fire within me that keeps it burning. I know that doubt is a part of the journey, but the belief in the light and the fire keeps me going.

Because, like a candle that has to burn to shed light, I know this: if I am to inspire, I have to keep burning. I have to remain centred, grounded, and thankful — and give it every ounce that I've got.

Not only for me.

But for every kid who looks on and aspires, every parent who quietly sacrifices, and every young sportsperson who feels overlooked, I do it for you. Your support and understanding make this journey worthwhile.

For every parent who quietly sacrifices.

For every young sportsperson who feels overlooked.

For all who still think that effort, discipline, and love for your nation count.

This journey isn't about sacrifice.

It's about service and duty. And I carry it with everything I've got.

Entry 21: The Ones Who Lit My Sky

They say no one walks alone. That's true. But I'll go one step further — no one *arrives* alone either.

Yes, I lace up the skates. I stand on the ice. I perform. But every step I've taken has been on the ground made firmer by the people who believed in me — not loudly, not dramatically, but in ways that mattered more.

Some of them — we've spoken about before. And yet, they remain too important not to name again, but this time, in a different light.

Mumma is the soil — grounding, giving, constant.

Papa is the sun — steady and strong, even when I don't look directly at him.

Archit Bhaiya and Suraj Bhaiya are like the wind—always behind me, moving me forward without asking for anything in return.

Sahney Sir is the mountain — firm, demanding, never moving — so I can learn to climb.

But this is not a story only about the people who stood with me. It's also about the people I lost along the way — the friends I lost, gradually, unintentionally, as my world started revolving around something greater than us.

Friendship means everything when you're growing up. It's where your laughter lives, where your secrets are stored. And sometimes, where your confidence begins.

I didn't always manage it well. I missed birthdays, skipped celebrations, and was gone without reason. As others navigated school dances, weekend games, and colony fun, I was elsewhere, attempting to execute a jump that might one day alter my future. They might have felt abandoned, left behind.

To any friend who I may have hurt — "I'm sorry."

I never stopped loving. I couldn't figure out how to say it. Or how to juggle it all. I hoped one day you'd see. That one day I'd be able to tell you that none of this was done to hurt you. I did everything I did with an eye on the future. Everything I did — I did thinking about the future. Not just my own but a future where I could also bring pride to my country. Because this journey, this life I'm building, has always been about more than me.

I've had to walk alone. There have been days when no one stood beside me, when applause went silent, and conversations faded. And in those moments, I've thought of what Rabindranath Tagore once said:

"Jodi tor daak shune keu na ashe, tobe ekla cholo re." *(If no one responds to your call — then go your own way alone.)*

And I have. I've kept walking — sometimes silently, sometimes shakily — trusting that someday, I'll have the chance to share my victories and my reasons.

One day, I hope the people who drifted away will see the complete picture. I wasn't chasing medals; I was chasing meaning. That what I gave wasn't to escape anyone — but to honour something larger.

I want to make history, be part of history and bring everyone—family, friends, mentors, and critics—into this shining story I'm trying to write. A story not of perfection but of purpose. Not of sacrifice but of service. If I can do that—even for one person or moment—then I've done something lasting.

Smiles, success, and skating at the Thailand Open Figure Skating Trophy 2024. A Moment of pride at the international stage !

Entry 22: The Language of Skating is Global

You can't fully comprehend it if you haven't lived it—the stress before a routine, the stillness that follows a fall, the weight of discipline when you're at practice once more and your friends are out having fun.

I was, therefore, relieved to learn that I was not alone when I encountered other young athletes living comparable lives. Finding like-minded individuals with whom I could discuss my challenges, fears, and experiences brought me great happiness.

Because tomorrow's routine had to be flawless, no one had to explain what it meant to train during festivals, travel exhausted, and miss birthday celebrations. They weren't just skaters. They served as mirrors, revealing aspects of myself that I had not previously noticed.

Not all of us spoke the same language. A few came from Thailand, and some from Malaysia, Japan, South Korea, and Indian cities like Chennai and Bengaluru. However, none of that mattered because skating, like music, doesn't need words.

It moves with grace, rhythm, timing, energy, and effort. You sense it. It's your life.

Additionally, we communicate effectively in the language of our common dreams when we skate together.

I developed more as a person and performer as I interacted with more skaters.

A boy from Kazakhstan once showed me how to make my arm movements smoother and more graceful while doing my footwork on the ice. A Bangalore girl assisted me in resolving a timing problem with my spin. A Japanese skater described how they see routines as musical narratives rather than sequences. None of this came from lessons. It resulted from living in the community, observing, inquiring, and sharing.

Without ever referring to it as such, we ended up teaching one another.

That is the strength of the athlete community I discovered. Through quiet belonging, not through coerced friendship. In this world, people give you feedback to help you succeed rather than to compete with you, where someone across the globe cheers for your reel.

Where someone you've never met says, "You made me start skating again."

Some of these relationships exist online — in messages, videos, voice notes left late at night, and skating reels. Others exist in rinks, in warm-up areas, in passing looks of comprehension.

But they're all living within me because each contributed something genuine.

Skating ought to be like this. Not a race or a lonely climb but a shared flight to success and fulfilment. Thus, we commemorate this every year on World Ice Skating Day, when rinks around the world come alive with activity and skaters of all skill levels unite to declare that we belong. World Ice Skating Day isn't just for professional skaters — it's for everyone. You'll see it all at places like Canada Square Park in Canary Wharf, London, Millcreek Common in Utah, or even the charming little setup in Mechelen, Belgium — from trained athletes to beginners. Some individuals make their first step onto the ice, holding onto the railing, laughing as they lose their balance, struggling to find their footing in rented skates. You spot little children tottering behind penguin instructors, couples gliding hand in hand, and visitors who happened by and thought they'd try it. No one's judging — everybody's just there. There's laughter, music, sometimes hot chocolate, and always this sense of warmth that says: you belong. And to be honest, that is the highlight of it all because skating on this day becomes not just about sport — it becomes about communal experience, communal joy. It's not about doing it correctly. It's about just attempting to. And I believe that is the loveliest form of community there is.

I celebrate the day in my way — sometimes with a quick ritual, sometimes by assisting someone younger, and sometimes simply by sharing with someone what ice skating has provided me.

Additionally, I frequently take part in skating seminars, training camps, and workshops hosted by organizations like iSKATE School and the Ice Skating Association of India (ISAI). Sometimes, I go there to learn — to improve my technique, understand new formats, and grow through feedback. However, I am frequently asked to speak and share my experience. I've talked to peers my age, kids younger than me, and even adults just starting in the sport. I consider these moments to be powerful for others and myself, whether through sharing mistakes, providing answers to questions, or just telling someone to keep going. Because every encounter serves as a reminder that my chosen path can lead to many opportunities for others, and that thought keeps me going. My aspiration today is to create space for more people here.

To share with every kid: you don't have to be perfect to get started. You have to start. Skating is not reserved for people who can already jump. It's for everyone who dreams of it. And with faith, determination, and support, even the tiniest dream can become unbreakable.

The community I discovered taught me this, and I wish to share it with others. We might be from different nations, cities, and situations, but when we skate, we're the same: young competitors attempting to shape something beautiful out of pressure and passion. So yes, I've found family along this road. But I've also identified a community—a group of skaters who travel with me without ever having to justify why.

And that's a special type of comfort —

The comfort of being seen.

The joy of being understood.

The promise of never having to dream alone again.

Entry 23: Built Different, Born Ready

Dear You,

You, who trains when others rest.

Who sacrifices when no one's watching.

Who's constantly told you're "too serious," "too ambitious," "too much."

Let me tell you right now — you are not too much. You are exactly enough. Let's get this straight — being different comes at a price. You're paying it in missed birthdays, skipped sleepovers, sore legs, tired eyes, and sometimes, silence. But you're not doing it for claps or likes. You're doing it because something inside you is burning — and you're brave enough to follow that fire.

There will be days when it sucks. When your body hurts, when you fall in front of everyone, when your friends stop calling because you're "never free." You'll see others chilling, laughing, scrolling — while you're stretching, sweating, doubting. And you'll wonder: *Is it worth it?* Yes. It is. Not because it's easy. Not because it's fair. But because it's yours.

Let me tell you something else. Even the sun — that massive ball of life-giving fire — gets criticised. When it shines too brightly in summer, people complain. They cover their eyes. They curse the heat. But come winter, they search for that same sun to feel alive again.

So be the sun. Shine anyway. Even when it makes people uncomfortable. Especially then.

You'll be judged, compared, and talked about, but don't shrink. Don't dim your light because some people can't handle the brightness.

Let them whisper. Let them doubt.

You? You focus. You build. You rise.

You'll be called "too much." Too quiet. Too focused. Too serious. Don't shrink. Don't soften your edges. You were not made to blend in. You were made to stand out — and that comes with noise, resistance, and, yes, a lot of falling. But falling isn't a failure. Think of the Phoenix — not just the mythical bird, but Fawkes from *Harry Potter*. Every time it burns, it is reborn. That's what you'll do. You'll burn in pressure, exhaustion, self-doubt — and then come back sharper, calmer, stronger. Burn, rebuild, come back stronger. Fall? Fine. Cry? Okay. But quit? Never.

You'll meet kids who trained with no coach. Athletes who practised on broken grounds. Champions who were told, "This isn't for girls" or "People like us don't make it big." They didn't wait for permission. And neither should you.

There's a whole world out there trying to water down your dreams. Don't let it.

Be loud about your ambition. Be obsessed. Be proud.

Yeah, you might not be at every party. But you'll be the reason people one day raise a toast.

You might not be in every group chat. But trust me — the ones who matter will notice when you step up.

One day, a kid will look at you and say, "I want to be like that."

And you'll know — every lonely evening, every tired morning, every ignored invite was worth it.

You're not weird. You're rare.

You're not falling behind. You're building ahead.

And you're not alone. You're just early.

So, if today feels hard, that's okay. Great things are built on hard days.

You've got this.

In fact — you've *always* had this.

Now go be fire.

Go be sunlight.

Go be *undeniable*.

— Someone who sees your fight and believes in your flight.

Entry 24: From Ice to Infinity

Most people believe the Olympic podium is the ultimate finish line. But for me, it's just a pause — a breath before the next big leap. Because when the cheering fades, and the anthem ends, my real work begins.

It's no longer just about my journey — it's about creating paths for others.

Before that, though, I have one very personal goal — to make it to the Junior Grand Prix and then the Senior Grand Prix. These are not just events. They are sacred milestones. The JGP and SGP are like the Oscars of our sport — where the best in the world come to compete and create history. I want to be one of them — to break records, raise the bar, and make figure skating in India synonymous with something strong, ambitious, and fearless.

I don't want to just appear on that stage — I want to redefine what an Indian skater can do because I've trained through heat, chaos, traffic, broken routines, and sore muscles, I've practised when the body said "no more." Although my parents supported me completely from the beginning when I showed interest in skating, I know that's not the reality for many children. In countless households, especially across India, when a child expresses a dream like this, the first response is often hesitation or a gentle "no." Many parents assume it's just a passing phase — that with age, the child will grow out of it. And for girls, the resistance can be even stronger. They're told, often without words, that sports or skating "aren't for them." But dreams don't come with age limits or gender labels. That belief needs to shift — because every child deserves the right to chase what makes them come alive. I still see children fighting with their parents or families who believe that "skating is not our thing." So when I step onto that ice, I'm not just skating for points — I'm skating for every child in India who dreams with no infrastructure, trains without resources, and hopes for a chance they're told doesn't exist.

Millions of children in my country feel this. Despite their raw talent, they're pulled back by a lack of access to training, facilities, and consistent support. And this is the wall I want to break. I want to use my journey, my story, and whatever platform I build to make skating a sport of the people—not privilege. That's why I felt something shift while watching *Skater Girl.* Directed by Manjari Makijany and co-written by her and Vinati Makijany, the film tells the story of a rural Indian girl discovering skateboarding against all odds. Starring Rachel Sanchita Gupta and Shafin Patel, released globally on June 11, 2021, by Netflix, walloped me. Because that film was more than entertainment — it was a mirror—a reflection of every unheard athlete, every unseen dream. And I knew then, louder than ever: *I want to be part of the change.*

When I look at my story — from skating on roller skates in Delhi to training on ice at the IWIS Center in Bangkok — I realize I didn't reach here alone. My coach, Sahney Sir's belief lifted me, my brother's quiet sacrifices, my parents' and grandparents' relentless support, and my teammates who clapped even when I stood up after a fall. Their love became my wings. I'm deeply grateful — not only to those who supported me but also to those who didn't. The ones who doubted, dismissed, or stayed silent pushed me in ways they'll never understand. Their disbelief became fuel. Their absence built resilience. Their harsh words taught me to listen less to noise and more to purpose. In many ways, they helped shape the strongest parts of me. And for that, I hold gratitude — quiet, unwavering, and growing every day.

Now, I want to be that for someone else. I want to coach — not just for routines, but for mindset. I want to be in rooms where policies are made. I want to help build programs, partner with the Ice Skating Association of India, support schools that introduce skating early, and bring certified coaching to districts and towns where no one has seen a pair of figure skates. I want to build rinks, launch scholarships, and make training accessible. Most of all, I want to ensure that no child—*no matter where they're from*—feels like they don't belong on the ice.

A medal is a moment, but what matters more is the movement you start. One day, I hope I'm sitting in an audience, watching a skater I once coached step onto a global stage. Maybe they'll be from a tiny village. Maybe they'll say, "I started because I saw him skate." And that's when I'll know: this was never just about my journey. It was always about everyone else I could bring along.

I'm not here to just collect trophies. I'm here to build a legacy.

To give what I was given.

And to be the reason that others believe.

Aarush gliding into greatness with style and confidence

Verses Kindler Publication

Verses Kindler Publication

Reach us through our website -

https://www.verseskindlerpublication.com/

For more information visit our

Instagram or Facebook page.